Grade Five Art Lessons: Table of Contents

GeoWat innovative teacher publishing © 2003

Learning Expectations with Art Activities

Knowledge of Elements	Corresponding Lesson
• Identify the three pairs of complementary colours;	• Complementary Colour Choice • Complementary Colour Study
• Identify warm and cool colours and develop an understanding of how they can be used to create a mood in a composition;	• Warm and Cool Perspective • Warm and Cool Sections • Warm and Cool Squared
• Describe how line may be used to define shapes and forms to create movements and depth;	• The Road to One Perspective • Sightless Contour Drawing • Shades and Tints • Monochromatic Style
▪ Identify how the shading of shapes can be used the create the illusion of depth;	• The Road to One Perspective • Monochromatic Style • Shading 3-D
• Identify tools used by artists to create the illusion of texture;	• Weaving Optical Illusions • Crayon Paper Batik • Mexican Mirror on the Wall • Squeegee Kids
• Develop an awareness and appreciation of Canadian Artist;	• Alex Janvier • Natur Ungalaq • Suzanne Brind'Amour

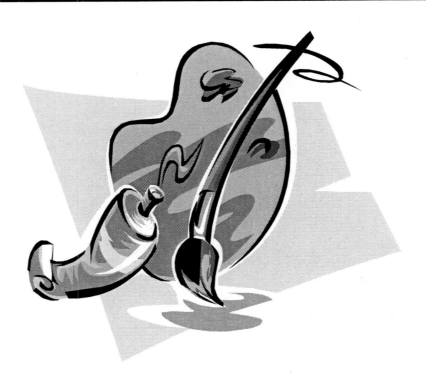

GeoWat innovative teacher publishing © 2003

Learning Expectations with Art Activities

Creative Work	Corresponding Lesson
• Organize their art to create an effect, using the elements of design;	• Dried Weed Display • Squared Off • Graduated Cut Outs • I Repeat, I Love You • Paper Cut Designs
▪ Produce two and three-dimensional work;	• Shading 3-D • Merry-go-round • Lantern Magic • Pin Art Luminaries • Honey Bee Good • Floating Ghosts • Button-eyed Fly • Pasta Twinkles • Japanese Carp Kites
▪ Identify strengths and area for improvement in their own work and that of others;	• Journal entries • Portfolio entries • Ongoing class discussion

Critical thinking	Corresponding lesson
▪ Use appropriate vocabulary;	• Journal entries • Portfolio entries • Ongoing class discussion.
▪ Defend their preference for a specific artwork with reference to at least three elements of design.	• Journal entries • Portfolio entries • Ongoing class discussion.
▪ Identify the role art plays in multicultural traditions.	• Mexican Mirror on the Wall • Aboriginal Leather Painting • Multicultural Holiday Crafts • Japanese Carp Kites • Chinese Scrolls • Egyptian Sarcophagi • Egyptian Tomb Paintings • Tet Blossoms • Rangoli From India • Huichol Paintings • Ceremonial Masks

Art Concepts Covered

Line:

Lines are a provocation to exploration. Lines may be straight, curved, jagged, broken, solid, horizontal, vertical, diagonal, fat, thin, regular, and irregular, long or short! Children develop an awareness of lines and suggested movement by working through the outlined activities. Encourage children to develop this awareness through activities such as weaving, sculpting, painting, and finger painting.

Shape:

The activities in this book will expose children to natural, symbolic, geometric and representational or abstract shapes found in their environment. The lessons include doing drawings based on outlines, modeling, sculpting, building with boxes, tubes or paper mache, painting and pattern making.

Colour:

The colour activities will introduce the children to tone, intensity, value, and paint consistency. The concepts of primary, secondary, warm, and cool colour relationships may also be taught through these lessons.

Texture:

The surface quality including appearance, tactile and visual effects may be explored through a number of the lessons in this book. Activities that involve the concept of texture include painting, weaving, sculpture, finger painting, paper mache, and fabric work.

Art Concepts Covered

Children learn art techniques through experimentation, demonstration, observation, and dialogue. Whenever possible, suggestions have been made to the teacher on how to include these concepts in the lessons.

Please remember that visual art techniques are not an end to themselves, but a means to develop the expression of ideas. It is necessary for children to have time to explore and use materials to practise the skills acquired.

Painting Skills:

Children should develop the following painting skills:

- how to put paint on the brush (paint should not spread onto the metal part of the brush);
- controlling paint (painting in large and small areas, varying the size of the lines);
- washing the brush before changing colours;
- mixing hues;
- painting next to dry and wet paint;
- painting over dry and wet paint;
- applying a wash;
- mixing tints and shades;
- blending colour;
- creating texture with paint;
- making smooth edges;
- combining paint and other media.

Pasting Skills

Apply bonding agents in a variety of ways, such as with brushes, applicators, fingers, toothpicks, scraps of paper, etc. Glue should not be visible on the finished product. Choosing a suitable adhesive as well as the placement and manipulation of the paste is a part of the skill development along with:

- applying small amounts of glue around the edges of the project;
- applying small amounts at strategic points on the project;
- applying glue to the shape not the background;
- applying pressure for a short time until the glue sticks.

Art Concepts Covered

Cutting or Tearing Skills:

Children should develop the following skills in the use of scissors:
- holding the scissors correctly;
- manipulating the paper and scissors;
- cutting a shape without the use of a pencil;
- cutting in even strokes;
- turning the paper to adapt to the scissors.

Tearing paper is different from ripping paper. When paper is ripped, it is an uncontrolled action. Tearing suggests control and the following techniques:
- using a short spreading movement to tear;
- or using the thumb and forefinger to tear.

Crayon and Stick Media:

Crayons, chalk, markers, oil pastels, and charcoal are only a few stick media, which can be:
- used heavily or lightly;
- blended, smeared, or dotted;
- polished, heated, ironed, or grooved;
- used under or over other media such as paint.

Modeling and Sculpting Materials

Various materials have been suggested for modeling and sculpting in this book. The teacher may also wish to change the medium to include some of the following suggestions:
- oil-based clay;
- water-based clay;
- starch & salt;
- paper mache;
- carving medium (mixing Plaster of Paris with sawdust, sand or vermiculite will make an excellent product for carving);
- card board box and tubes;
- sawdust and paste.

Vocabulary and Definitions

Advancing Colours: These colours seem to jump to the front of a painting. They are warm or vivid colours such as reds and yellows.

Black: The colour black is the absence of light. Paint pigment called black actually has other colours such as blue or brown added to it. Adding black to a colour may make it appear dull.

Blending: May be the mixing two or more colours together, or creating a gradual change between colours.

Burnishing: Polishing or compressing the colour. Burnishing in coloured pencil drawings may be accomplished with a white pencil (or lighter colour of the colour being used) and rubbing over the area. This will iron out the grain of the paper compressing the pigment, to create a slight shine on the surface. Burnishing increasing the brilliance of the colours.

Collage: Creating a picture by gluing pieces of materials such as paper, photos, magazine clippings, or found objects, to a flat surface.

Colour: The eye sees colour when light bounces off an object. The "properties" of colour are hue, saturation, value and temperature.

Complementary Colours: Complementary colours are colours opposite each other on the colour wheel. For example: yellow and violet.

Composition: Compositions are a balance of positive and negative spaces. Interesting compositions may be created by varying the shapes, textures and values.

Contrast: May be achieved by placing opposites beside one another. (rough/smooth, light/dark complementary colours)

Cool colours: Soothing colours such as greens, blues and violets are considered cool colours. They seem to retreat into the background or distance.

Crosshatching: Volume or shading in a picture may be created by drawing lines crossing each other in different directions. The closer the lines, the darker the shading.

Drybrush: Pulling the paint out of the brush by dabbing on a paper towel, or similar surface before painting will causes the brush to skip on the surface of the paper or canvas producing a broken effect. This is particularly good for creating the look of wood or texture.

Frottage: From the French word "frotter" to rub. Texture is created when paper is placed over a textured surface and rubbed with a pencil, pastel, etc. causing the texture to be reproduced on the surface of the paper. Often called a rubbing!

Vocabulary and Definitions

Highlights: Small light areas can add the finishing touch to a painting, and make it look professional. The sparkle on water, sunlight on the edges of a house or snow on a rooftop make the painting come to life!

Monochromatic: A painting done in different shades and tints of one colour.

Pointillism: A style of painting commonly attributed to Georges Seurat it is created when small dots of colour are placed close together. From a distance, the dots disappear and the colours blend.

Primary Colours: These are the basic colours red, blue and yellow from which all other colours can be mixed. Mixtures of these produce the secondary colours orange, green and violet.

Secondary Colours: These are colours produced from the mixture of even amounts of two primary colours. Blue and red produces violet, yellow and red makes orange, and blue and yellow makes green.

Sgraffito: A technique created by scratching into paint to reveal the colours underneath.

Tertiary Colours: These are colours produced by mixing primary colours with secondary colours.

Wash: Is created by adding water to paint making it thin enough to allow colours applied underneath to show through.

Warm Colours: The colours in the yellow to red range are considered warm colours. They make us think of such things as the sun and fire. Warm colours are used to make an object appear to advance into the foreground.

About Picture Making Skills

Picture making is an excellent form of art expression. Give children regular opportunities to develop their abilities. Motivation for picture making may come from several sources at once, including children's sensory perceptions, feelings, experiences, ideas, tools, materials, and theme suggestions from the teacher.

Interesting materials with which to paint:

- Fingers
- Branches
- Rags
- Brushes
- Plastic pot scrubbers
- Sticks
- Rope
- Sponges
- Cotton swabs
- Cork
- Blocks of wood
- Feathers
- Toothpicks
- Cotton balls
- Foam

Interesting tools with which to draw:

- Crayons
- Chalk
- Felt tip markers
- Pencils
- Charcoal
- Make up
- Fingers
- Ink pen
- Pencil crayons

Interesting surfaces on which to paint or draw:

- Newsprint
- Tissue paper
- Glass (windows)
- Plastic wrap
- Aluminum foil
- Paper plates
- Paper bags
- Cardboard
- Paper towels
- Stones
- Blocks of wood
- Crepe paper
- Cloth
- Waxed paper
- Foam

Suggestions on how to organize a picture-making centre:

- Permit time for the activity;
- Some activities may need more than one class depending on the students and the schedule;
- Have children work in groups. Four is a practical number;
- Assign "job numbers" to each member of the group;
- Keep work where children will be able to allow it to dry, and reclaim it easily (Clothes lines of string with pegs make it easy for young children to hang their paintings to dry).

How To Organize Your Classroom For Art Instruction

Physical Set Up:

Organize the classroom to allow for storage and work areas.

- Positions storage areas so that children can find and return supplies;

- Water tins are a part of cleanup in a paint area so a rational place for the paint area would be close to a sink. If a sink is not available, an area of the floor or table may be covered with newspaper or plastic drop sheets and a bucket of water may be used for cleaning;

- Turn up rinsed water tins on a pad of newspaper and allow to dry to prevent rusting;

- Store brushes with the bristles up to prevent distortion, by placing them in a tall empty juice can;

- If cupboards are not available to store paints, consider a large plastic milk bin or cardboard box;

How To Organize Your Classroom For Art Instruction

Supplies and Materials:

Encourage children to experiment with a variety of media, materials, and tools. Teach lessons on how to care for and maintain the equipment as well as organize it. The following is a list of suggested materials needed for a good visual arts program:

- **crayons:**   Try to provide a variety of sizes, as well as other stick materials such as oil pastels, markers, coloured pencils, and charcoal;

- **paper:**   A variety of papers about 45 cm. X 60 cm. should be used. Manila and newsprint are some types of paper recommended. Other papers such as craft paper, finger painting paper, construction paper or corrugated paper may be suggested in the materials lists;

- **scissors:**   A good set of scissors is necessary for facility of cutting. Points of the scissors should be rounded, and a few left handed pairs should be available;

- **paint:**   Water-based tempera is used most often. Mixing a small amount of dish detergent into the paint will make it easier to wash out of clothing;

- **brushes:**   Generally a 1.5 cm. brush is used for projects, but students should have access to a variety of sizes and shapes to apply paint in lines, large masses, patterns or textures;

- **other media:**   Be innovative in allowing children to experiment with natural and found materials such as twigs, leaves, stones, cloth, cardboard, foam, and commercial materials such as wool, wire, toothpicks, plastiscene, finger-paint, burlap, etc.

How To Organize Your Classroom For Art Instruction

Before Beginning a Visual Arts Lesson:

- Assemble the materials and supplies necessary for the lesson;
- Have the children arrange their desks, or tables in groups of four (it may be necessary to allow some children to work on the floor);
- When the time comes, have the children distribute supplies according to their "job numbers".

Routines:

The emphasis should be on an orderly and well-organized distribution and set-up. The participation of students in as many of the responsibilities as possible is optimal. The children should understand the expectations and be involved in the routines of clean-up and organization.

Distribution of Materials:

Assign each child or member of a group a "job number" so that they may have a specific chore to do during set up and clean up time. For example:

- number one will get the newspaper and put it away;
- number two will get the water and pour it out after art time;
- number three will get the brushes and clean the brushes;
- number four will get the drawing paper and collect finished work.

Clean-up:

- Usually ten minutes is enough time to allow for clean-up, depending on the age and motivation of the group;
- Place an emphasis on orderliness and the development of useful work habits.
- Children should assume total responsibility for clean up.

Art Centres

In order to run successful visual arts centres, good planning on the part of the teacher is essential. Follow these steps:

FIRST: Examine your timetable and decide on one time block to devote consistently as art centres time.

SECOND: Decide how many centres will be set up during art centres and what they will be.

THIRD: Store what is needed for each activity in their individual bin. In this way, centres are organized and ready to go. Each centre bin should include:
- All materials needed to complete the activity for each child;
- A sample of completed work to show students.

FOURTH: Introduce and explain the expectation of each learning centre to the class. This is the time to teach any specific skills, needed to complete a centre. In addition, review how many students are allowed at each centre.

If a learning centre approach is new to your classroom, balance your centres so that some of the activities will need minimum teacher direction, such as a free exploration painting centre. This will allow students an opportunity to learn how to work independently and with other students.

Check Points for Teachers:

☑   Encourage children to do their own work;
☑   Exhibit all of the children's work;
☑   Encourage children to be inventive;
☑   Encourage children to finish their work;
☑   Encourage children to talk about their work using art vocabulary;
☑   Provide ample time and opportunity for art;
☑   Teach children to care for materials;
☑   Encourage children to experiment with various media;
☑   Encourage children to be observant and aware of their environment;
☑   Be enthusiastic and have fun!

There is no right or wrong!

What kind of paper?

There are several different types of paper, from the common computer print-out paper, to the lovely Japanese rice papers. How can you decide what paper is the right type for the project on which you are embarking? Here are few definitions that may help:

Cartridge Paper:
- use with inks or pastels
- heavier than photocopy paper
- slightly rougher surface to "grab" medium
- can withstand wet

Tissue Paper:
- thin
- polished surface
- transparent
- bleeds when wet
- fragile

Watercolour Paper:
- specially formulated to withstand wet
- needs to be taped down to prevent warping
- comes in different weights (40 lbs. will suit most purposes)
- cold press has rougher surface
- hot press allows watercolour to float on surface for longer times

Newsprint:
- thin
- use for projects that do not require permanence
- absorbs inks and water easily
- is newspaper before the printing
- good for the last layer of a paper mache project

Rice paper:
- usually expensive
- used in projects that require strength
- usually can be recognized by a fibre-like thread through paper

Did you know...

- Mixing 1 part white glue and 1 part tempera paint will give the paint a shiny wet look?

- 2 parts white glue 1 part liquid starch makes silly dough?

- 2 teaspoons of salt mixed with 1 teaspoon of liquid starch makes icy pictures?

- Egg yolks, dry detergent and food colouring makes a paint that will stick to any surface?

- Mixing equal parts of liquid starch and cold water makes an excellent paper mache glue?

- You can make bakers clay by mixing 2 cups of flour, 1 cup of salt and water, and baking at 300 degrees?

- To make no bake dough that stays soft, use the above recipe but add 2 tablespoons of oil?

- Corn syrup painted over a surface gives a shiny, leathery, golden finish? (May take a long time to dry on humid days!)

- To make tempera paint brighter and easier to wash out, add liquid starch and liquid soap in a 2:1 ratio?

- To dye pasta quickly and make bright colours, pour a small amount of rubbing alcohol into the food colouring before dropping in the uncooked pasta?

September Art Lessons

Try these art centres:

❖ Apply chalk around the edges of a fall leaf. Use a tissue to rub a misty area around the edges of the leaf.

❖ Trace a classroom object, such as scissors, overlapping to make an interesting design. Colour positive and negative spaces different shades.

❖ Make a colour tone scene by gluing warm colours on cool colours. (Red on blue, etc.)

❖ Curl shades of one colour of paper strips around a pencil. Arrange the curls progressing from light to dark.

❖ Draw "waves" from left to right across white paper. Colour each area between the waves different colours.

❖ Tear tissue paper into leaf shapes and dampen. Place along a painted branch. When dry, remove the tissue paper, leaving a print behind.

❖ Make a garland of leaves, fruit or vegetables to drape around the room.

GeoWat innovative teacher publishing © 2003

Dried Weed Display

Time Frame: 40 minutes

MOTIVATION:

When fall has set in, many wild plants make a beautiful arrangement. Display a collection of wild plants on the bulletin board using this clever activity.

MOTIVATION:

- Construction paper
- Dried weeds collected over the fall
- Wool or yarn
- Fabric scraps (optional)
- Glue
- Scissors

WHAT TO DO:

1. Demonstrate for the children how to cut the weeds into desirable lengths and trim off unwanted leaves and branches;
2. Cut a piece of construction paper in a large "U" shape;
3. If using fabric scraps, decorate this large "U", making a "pocket";
4. If not using fabric scraps, have children draw patchwork designs on the construction paper;
5. Glue the "U" to another piece of construction paper;
6. Arrange the dried weeds in the pocket;
7. Mount the pockets on the bulletin board!

Squared Off

Time Frame: 40 minutes

MOTIVATION:
When children are getting to know each other at the beginning of the year, this activity helps them share their "specialness".

MATERIALS:
- 6 square pieces of drawing paper
- Colouring materials (markers, coloured pencils, crayons, etc.)
- Transparent tape
- Magazines (optional)

WHAT TO DO:
1. Brainstorm with the children words that describe their personal attributes;
2. Demonstrate how to draw these attributes in bubble letters, or similar large style writing on the square pieces of drawing paper;
3. Be sure to tell the children to add their name;
4. Using the magazines (optional) have the children find pictures that represent them, and glue onto the squares;
5. Assemble the squares into a cube;
6. Hang the cubes from the classroom ceiling.

Shades & Tints

Time Frame: 40 minutes

MOTIVATION:

Value is the intensity or lightness and darkness of a color. Ways of showing colour value may be achieved by pressure on the coloured pencil, or by adding black or white over the top. Blending colours achieves another value.

MATERIALS:

- Drawing paper
- Colouring pencils crayons

WHAT TO DO:

1. Demonstrate for the children how to draw "swatches" of colour using one pencil crayon. Explain that as each swatch is coloured, more pressure is applied, changing the value of the colour;
2. To create darker values, demonstrate for the children how colouring over top of the coloured swatch with a black pencil crayon will create deeper shades, while adding white will create lighter shades;
3. Distribute drawing paper and ask children to create a line design;
4. Allow the children to experiment by combining colours and adding black and white to fill in the line designs.

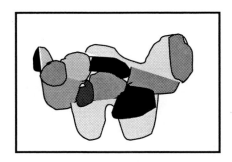

Warm and Cool Perspective

Time Frame: 40 minutes

MOTIVATION:

In this easy lesson, children will clearly see how colour affects perspective. It is also a good opportunity to review tonality of colour, or how a colour changes with the addition of black or white.

MATERIALS:

- Materials:
- White paper
- Tempera paint
- Brushes
- Water
- Pencils
- Bright yellow construction paper
- Glue

WHAT TO DO:

1. Demonstrate for the children how to fold their paper into 4 sections;
2. Using a pencil, lightly draw a skyline (it should look like roof tops, with rectangular, triangular, square, and semi-circular shapes) across the first section;
3. Repeat this skyline in each of the four sections;
4. Have the children choose one colour to work with and demonstrate how to mix black into the colour, making it very dark;
5. Paint the first skyline in this colour;
6. Move to the next skyline and adding less black to the colour, paint the second skyline;
7. In the next block, add a small amount of white to the colour, and paint the third skyline;
8. In the last block mix white into the colour, making it very light;
9. Paint the sections above the skylines (the triangles, squares, etc.) in black;
10. Using the bright yellow paper glue small rectangles or squares on the "buildings" to represent the windows.

DISCUSSION: Ask the children what effect the different tones have on the picture. (Things seem lighter the further away they are.)

Warm and Cool Sections

Time Frame: 40 minutes

MOTIVATION:

Colour is often associated with moods or language. "Red hot" or "blue mood". Warm colours are red, orange, or yellow. Cool colours are blue, purple or green. This activity will demonstrate warm and cool colours.

MATERIALS:

- Crayons or coloured pencils
- Drawing paper

WHAT TO DO:

1. Demonstrate for the children how to fold the paper in an accordion pleat or fan;
2. On the first section of the fan, colour designs or patterns in cool colours (blues, greens, purples, etc.);
3. On the next section, colour designs or patterns in warm colours (reds, yellows, oranges, etc.);
4. Stand the finished fan on the desk. As the students look from one side of the fan, they will see only cool colours. From the other side the students will see only warm colours.

DISCUSSION:

Think of some names to call new colours that might be invented. For instance "apple bruise brown" or "banana split yellow!"

Warm and Cool Squared

Time Frame: 40 minutes

MOTIVATION:

Once the children have been introduced to the concepts of warm and cool colours, this activity is fun and simple.

MATERIALS:

- Graphing paper with large squares
- Warm and cool colouring materials
- Pencil

WHAT TO DO:

1. Demonstrate for the children how to sketch a simple shape on the graph paper;
2. Decide if the area inside the sketch will be warm or cool;
3. Decide if the area outside the sketch will be warm or cool;
4. Colour each square a different shade, according to the decisions that were made. If warm colours are to be used outside the sketch, colour all the squares outside a different warm shade.

VARIATION:

On large squared graph paper, colour each square a different colour or design.

October Lessons

Try these art centres:

- ❖ Make an observational drawing of pumpkin.

- ❖ Colour glue with food colouring. Draw on plastic wrap with the coloured glue. Place a second piece of wrap on top and squish together. Cut black construction paper into a frame and place squished art into the frame. Trim plastic wrap to fit.

- ❖ Make a daylight scene by gluing black silhouettes on white paper.

- ❖ Paint or colour a picture using only shades of orange and black.

- ❖ Twist green tissue paper into "vines" and glue on "pumpkins".

- ❖ Fold paper towels in different configurations. (fan, triangle, etc.) Dampen paper and dip into different coloured paint. Refold and dip again. Dry and unfold.

GeoWat innovative teacher publishing © 2003

Halloween Activities

Black Magic Etchings

Create a spooky night etching. Have children colour broad bands of colour using crayons on a piece of paper. Encourage children to apply pressure on the crayons. Mix a tablespoon of dishwashing detergent into black tempera paint. Have children paint over their entire paper with the black mixture. Once the paint is dry, children may make spooky etchings using Popsicle sticks, coins, or old ballpoint pens.

Garlands of Ghosts, Bats and Pumpkins

Have children trace and cut out ghost, bat, and pumpkin shapes from black, orange, and white construction paper. Make the shapes appear to be three-dimensional by slitting one shape from the bottom and one shape from the top. Slide the shapes together.

Black Bats Across the Moon

Create a silhouettes of a bats using black construction paper, circles for the bodies, smaller circles for the heads, and wing shapes. Glue the silhouettes on a large yellow circle to represent a full moon. Encourage children to write a story about their bats.

Face Painting

Create easy washable face paint by mixing hand soap and tempera paint. Apply the face paint with cotton swabs.
KEEP THE FACE PAINT AWAY FROM EYES AND MOUTH!

Corn Harvests

Time Frame: 40 minutes

MOTIVATION:
Celebrate Thanksgiving by harvesting Indian corn. This colourful corn can be simulated in this quick and effective activity.

MATERIALS:
- Bristol board
- 3cm. Squares of tissue paper in black, yellow, orange, and brown
- Glue
- Scissors
- Brown paper

WHAT TO DO:
1. Demonstrate for the children how to draw a cob-shape on the Bristol board;
2. Scrunch the pieces of tissue paper into rolls;
3. Glue the wads of tissue paper onto the cob shape;
4. Using the brown paper, create "husks" to attach to the ends of the corn;
5. Decorate the classroom door with the Indian corn cobs!

 **TEACHER TIP:** Recycle paper lunch bags to use as the "husks".

Floating Ghosts

Time frame: two 40 minute periods

MOTIVATION:

Halloween is a time for fun and fantasy. In this activity, a variation on paper mache will make a ghosts that seems to float when hung from a tree or ceiling.

MATERIALS:

- Styrofoam coffee cup
- Plastic film wrap
- newspaper
- White glue
- Masking tape
- Spray bottle
- Paper towel, or toilet paper, or tissue paper

WHAT TO DO:

1. Demonstrate for the children how to make a frame from the coffee cup and newspaper;
2. Tape the coffee cup to the table in order to make it stable;
3. Make a ball from a sheet of newspaper and attach it to the top of the coffee cup using masking tape;
4. Tape two oval shapes stretched out at the sides for arms;
5. Cover the shape with plastic wrap, allowing the plastic wrap to droop over the arms and onto the table;
6. Using a mixture of 1 part glue to 3 parts water, fill the spray bottle;
7. Spray the plastic wrap with the watered down glue mixture;
8. Drape strips of the paper towel (or other chosen from the list) over the glued plastic wrap;
9. Gently mold the paper towel into a ghostly shape, allowing some of the paper towel to drape onto the table;
10. Apply at least three coats of paper towel to the sculpture;
11. Allow to dry;
12. Carefully peel off the coffee cup and add scary eyes and mouth details;
13. Hang to impress visitors!

Lantern Magic

Time frame: 40 minutes

MOTIVATION:

Using wax paper to press leaves or other natural objects is not a new concept, but shaping them into lanterns makes it see-through magic!

MATERIALS:

- Wax paper
- Construction paper
- Fall leaves in bright autumn colours
- Stapler
- Iron
- Newspaper

WHAT TO DO:

1. Demonstrate for the children how to arrange the collection of fall leaves on one piece of wax paper;
2. Place a second sheet of wax paper over the leaves;
3. The teacher should iron the sheets, sealing the leaves between the wax paper;
4. Have the children staple strips of construction paper on the top and bottom of the wax paper sheets;
5. Roll the sheets into a tube and staple;
6. Add a strip of construction paper across the top to make a handle;
7. Hang the attractive fall lantern!

Halloween Sunsets

Time frame: 40 minutes

MOTIVATION:

Sponge painting can create an effective background for a silhouette picture. In this activity, orange and yellow were chosen as the background colour, but choosing a different background colour, can alter the mood of the picture.

MATERIALS:

- Drawing paper
- Orange and yellow tempera paint
- Black construction paper
- Scissors
- Sponges
- White wax crayon
- Glue

WHAT TO DO:

1. Brainstorm with the children various Halloween symbols; (black cats, bats, witches, pumpkins, etc.)
2. Demonstrate for the children how to draw a large moon in one area of the drawing paper using the white crayon;
3. Dip a sponge into yellow and orange paint and streak the paint across the drawing paper;
4. Continue to fill the drawing paper with the paint streaked horizontally across the paper;
5. While the paint is drying direct the children to cut Halloween symbols of their choice from black construction paper. Encourage the children to keep the cut outs simple;
6. Cut long strips of black construction paper to simulate a fence;
7. Once the background is dry, glue the silhouettes to the drawing paper, creating a sunset silhouette!

DISCUSSION:

How can this technique be applied to other pictures?

Pinecone Turkey 'Toons

Time Frame: 40 minutes

MOTIVATION:
Thanksgiving is a time of festive turkeys! In this activity, pinecone pieces are used to create a turkey to be proud of!

MATERIALS:
- Glue
- Pinecones
- Markers

WHAT TO DO:
1. Demonstrate for the children how to peel apart the pinecones, separating the scales;
2. Using the pinecone scales, create the feathers for the turkey, by laying rows in an arch;
3. Draw a turkey head and body in the centre of the arch;
4. Repeat the picture, making another turkey facing the first;
5. Design a cartoon caption for the image!

November Art Lessons

Try these art centres:

❖ Make an observational drawing of a hand.

❖ Drop blobs of paint on paper. Using spray bottles, spray with water from different distances.

❖ Place a piece of paper in the bottom of a shoebox. Drop blobs of paint onto the paint and roll a marble through the paint making tracks on the white paper.

❖ Roll out a large piece of paper and have 5 children on a signal, rotate around the paper, painting as they go!

❖ Tack long strips of black construction paper over murals to make it appear as if you are looking through a window.

❖ Practise colouring a colouring page on different surfaces, such as sandpaper to create texture.

Mexican Mirror On the Wall!

Time Frame: 40 minutes

MOTIVATION:

If you visit Mexico, you may have the pleasure of seeing yourself in an ornately decorated mirror, common in Mexico. Using yarn and aluminum foil, this activity reproduces the look of an accent mirror.

MATERIALS:

- Glue
- Scissors
- Wool or yarn in various thickness and colours
- Bristol board
- Aluminum foil

WHAT TO DO:

1. Demonstrate for the children how to make a large oval or square on the Bristol board;
2. Cut a piece of aluminum foil to fit in the middle of the Bristol board;
3. Glue in place;
4. Leaving an opening in the centre where the aluminum foil has been glued;
5. Spread the glue on a small space around the Bristol board;
6. Press the yarn or wool into the glue;
7. Explain to the children they should vary the direction, thickness and colour of the yarn or wool.

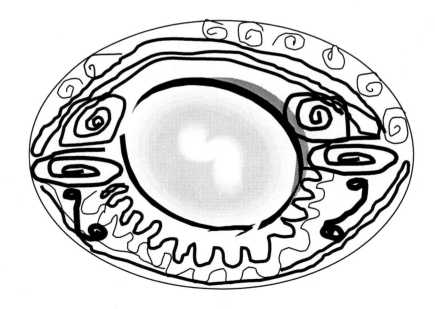

Michelangelo di Lodovico Buonarroti Simoni

Time Frame: 40 minutes

MOTIVATION:

Michelangleo di Lodovico Buonarroti Simoni (1475-1564) was an Italian sculptor, painter, architect, and poet who had a profound influence on Western art. Michelangelo, known for his work on the Sistine Chapel of the Vatican painted from 1508-1512. This great Renaissance artist painted the ceiling while lying on his back. To see examples of Michelangelo's work, go to: www.ibiblio.org/wm/paint/auth/michelangelo/

MATERIALS:

- Drawing paper
- Paint (paint should be thick and not drip)
- Brushes
- Water
- Masking tape
- Table or desk
- Smock to be worn by painter!

WHAT TO DO:

1. Demonstrate for the children how to sketch the form of a person on the drawing paper;
2. When the sketch is to the satisfaction of the teacher and child, have child lie on his/her back under a table or desk;
3. Tape sketch to the underside of the table or desk;
4. Using the thickened paint, have children paint their sketches.

TEACHER TIP: To thicken paint, add white glue or flour.

Weaving Optical Illusions

Time Frame: 40 minutes

MOTIVATION:

In this activity children will create an optical illusion using magazine cut outs.

MATERIALS:

- Magazines
- Glue
- Scissors
- Pencil
- Ruler
- Construction paper

WHAT TO DO:

1. Have the children flip through the magazines to find an action picture;
2. Show the children how to draw lightly around the picture on the construction paper;
3. Using a ruler, draw another line around the top and bottom of the of the picture outline about 2 cm. thick;
4. Demonstrate for the children how to draw straight lines about 2 cm. thick vertically across the picture;
5. Cut on the lines;
6. Glue the first strip aligning the top portion of the strip with the top line on the construction paper;
7. Aligning the second strip on the bottom line of the construction paper;
8. Assemble the picture but stagger each strip aligning with the upper and bottom lines of the construction paper.

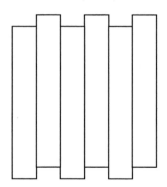

Alex Janvier

The First Nations People of Canada have been creating art for many, many years. When non-native people came to North America, they collected and traded tools made by native people. The non-native people did not always understand the beauty of the Native Art, but artists like Alex Janvier helped to make Native Art an important part of Canada.

Alex Janvier was born in 1935. He was raised on the Le Goffe Reserve in Cold Lake Alberta. He studied at the Alberta College of Art and graduated in 1960. Alex Janvier paints pictures that seem to flow across the canvas. He likes to draw about the traditional native beadwork designs and many of the things that have happened to the First Nations people in Canada when he paints. You can see examples of his art at www.mcmichael.com

Many beautiful designs are found in Native beadwork. Porcupine quills were dyed and sewn to leather bands or birch bark. Use the following activity to create designs that emulate this beadwork.

Beadwork Designs

MATERIALS:

- Flat toothpicks
- Food colouring or jelly powder crystals (added to small quantities of water to create a dye bath for the toothpicks).
- Glue
- Strips of brown construction paper (bracelets)

WHAT TO DO:

1. Before beginning the activity, soak the toothpicks in food colouring or diluted jelly powder bath;
2. Allow toothpicks to dry;
3. After viewing examples of native beadwork, distribute strips of brown construction paper to be used as bracelets;
4. Model for the children how to create a design on their construction paper, like a bird, tree or any traditional native picture by breaking the toothpicks to fit the design;
5. Next have children glue toothpick pieces making the design using colours of their choice;
6. The teacher may wish to read with the class several native stories and legends to act as inspiration for the children.

Teacher Tip: Lay toothpicks across the construction paper bracelets so when bent around the wrist, the toothpicks will not break.

Find legends at: http://www.ainc-inac.gc.ca/ks/english/index_e.html

Aboriginal Leather Paintings

Time Frame: 40 minutes

MOTIVATION:

In this activity students can recreate the leather porcupine quill designs of the First Nations people. Use this lesson after children have been exposed to the bead work of artists such as Alex Janvier at: www.mcmichael.com

MATERIALS:

- Brown paper bags
- Water
- Crayons

WHAT TO DO:

1. Before beginning this activity, have the children soak paper lunch bags in water;
2. Carefully squeeze the excess water out of the bag;
3. Smooth out the paper bag and let dry;
4. Once dry, transfer beadwork designs onto the brown paper bag;
5. Rip fringe on the sides of the paper;
6. Use as teepees, headbands, or other native accessory.

December Art Lessons

Try these art centres:

❖ Candy cane mice are nice! On the straight end of a candy cane, glue a fluffy cotton ball or pompom. Glue on pink felt ears, whiskers from pipe cleaners, and googly eyes. The candy cane makes the tail!

❖ Paint a picture using a pine branch with lots of pine needles for a brush.

❖ Cut 4 circles of wrapping paper, wallpaper or foil. Push a brad tack thought the centre and cut fringes around the edges. Carefully pull apart to make an ornament.

❖ Paint on wax paper. Take a print from the painting by pressing drawing paper over top of the wax paper.

❖ Make a sparkling collage from aluminum foil, tinsel, and glitter.

❖ Cut pines cones in cross sections and paint and roll in glitter to make tree decorations.

Multicultural Holiday Crafts

Hanukkah Stars

Provide children with an outline of a Star of David. Crunch up aluminum foil to crinkle, and unfold to flatten. Cut the aluminum foil in the shape of the Star of David and glue onto blue construction paper. Cut around the shape leaving a border around the star. Colour over the foil with markers, to create a stained glass look.

Kwanzaa Prints

Kwanzaa, Swahili for "first fruit", is a traditional African festival that lasts seven days starting on the twenty-sixth of December. Using green, red, yellow, blue and black paint pads, demonstrate for the children how to use fruit cut into stamps to create various fruit print patterns.

Ramadan Silhouettes

On wet Manila paper, have children create a dawn or dusk effect by applying streaks of yellow, orange and pink paint on the whole paper. Let the paper dry. Meanwhile have children cut out silhouettes of mosques and other buildings found in the community. Paste these silhouettes on the dry dusk or dawn paintings.

Holiday Wreath

Glue five small pretzels in a circle. Glue five more pretzels overlapping the first row. Paint with 1 part glue 1 part water to seal. Weave a colourful ribbon through the pretzels.

Ice Cream Cone Christmas Trees

Have children place an ice cream cone upside down on a paper plate. This will be the Christmas tree. Cover the cone with green frosting or green coloured whipped cream. Decorate the ice cream cone Christmas tree with assorted candies.

Pasta Twinkles

Time Frame: 40 minutes

MOTIVATION:

Snowflakes can conjure up shivers or pleasant memories of decorations on a tree. Try these creations to make a unique blizzard!

MATERIALS:

- Wheel and shell-shaped pasta
- Glue
- Wax paper
- Fishing line
- Glitter

WHAT TO DO:

1. Demonstrate for the children how to dip the flat side of a pasta wheel into the glue;
2. Place the pasta wheels in a circle making sure each side of the wheel touches the next one;
3. Fill in the middle space with a wheel;
4. Attach more wheels at the area of the joints in the circle of wheels;
5. To each of these wheels, add a shell-shaped pasta;
6. Allow the glue to dry;
7. Spread a thin coat of glue over the pasta flake and shake on glitter;
8. Peel from the wax paper and hang with fishing line.

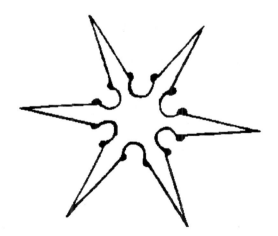

Squeegee Kids

Time Frame: 40 minutes

MOTIVATION:

Experimenting with colour is always fun. In this activity, children will witness the blending and bleeding of colour.

MATERIALS:

- Food colouring
- Squeegee
- Copy paper (or other paper that is not too porous)

WHAT TO DO:

1. Demonstrate for the children how to make a puddle of food colouring across the top of the paper;
2. Using the squeegee, carefully pull the colour across the page;
3. Experiments with pulling the squeegee in different patterns, such as wavy, swirling, etc.;
4. Allow the page to dry, and use for seasonal decorations such as Christmas wrapping paper, Easter egg shapes, rainbows, flowers, planets, etc.

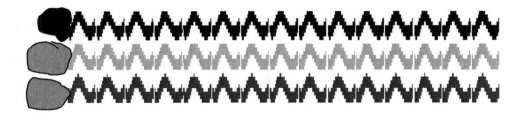

 # Natar Ungalaq

Natar Ungalaq was born in Nunavut in 1959. At nine years old he began to carve stone. He watched the older stone carvers and learned how to create sculptures out of soft soapstone. His work has been featured throughout Canada, Washington D.C. and Italy and Germany. You can see his art at the Art gallery of Ontario and in the National Gallery of Canada.

Animal Carvings

Time Frame: 40 minutes

MOTIVATION:

This activity can be incorporated in a study of Canada's north or as a study of Inuit carvers.

MATERIALS:

- Clay (approximately a 5 inch cube for each student)
- Paper clips bent open to allow carving with a loop
- Water

WHAT TO DO:

1. Demonstrate for the children how to soften the clay by manipulating and pounding;
2. Help children to visualize a creature in their clay shape;
3. Using the open paper clip as a tool, carve away the clay to shape the animal;
4. Dip fingers into the water and smooth over rough clay.

Complementary Colour Study

Time Frame: Two 40 minutes

Use this sheet to create a colour palette an artist would use to learn about colours and how they mix. Colour each area, overlapping and blending between the colours. Complementary colours are opposite each other on the colour wheel.

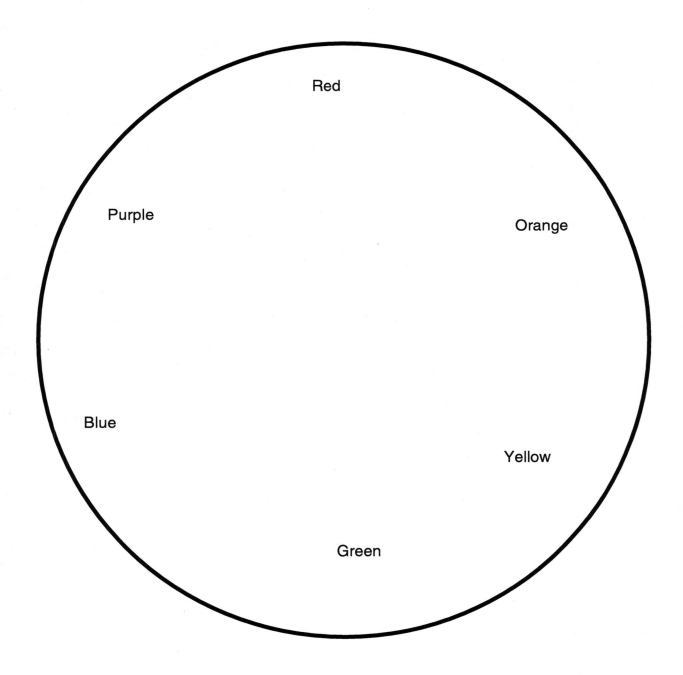

JANUARY LESSONS

Try these art centres:

- ❖ Make an observational drawing of a pop can.

- ❖ Try sculpturing with tin foil. Twist and bend the foil into interesting shapes.

- ❖ Make a quick diorama by cutting the centre out of a paper plate and building the diorama in another. Staple the two paper plates together.

- ❖ Draw a picture using chalk on wet paper.

- ❖ Practise filling in sections of a colouring page using tiny pieces of torn construction paper.

- ❖ Create a picture using puffy materials, like foam packing peanuts, fiberfill, or cotton puffs.

- ❖ Use a pastry brush to paint a design.

Egyptian Sarcophagi

Time Frame: Two 40 minute periods

MOTIVATION:

When studying the culture of ancient Egypt, introduce the subject of mummies and their tombs or sarcophagi.   Aliki has written a book *Mummies Made in Egypt,* an excellent preface to this activity. It has also been made into a Reading Rainbow video. Be sure to highlight the techniques used in the decorative details on the sarcophagi.

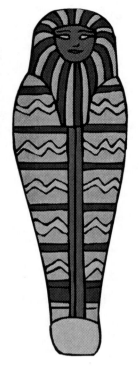

MATERIALS:

- Materials:
- Newsprint
- Newspaper
- White glue
- Water
- Paints
- Paintbrushes
- Aluminum foil

WHAT TO DO:

1. Demonstrate for the children, how to mould using the aluminum foil as a modeling compound, the shape a sarcophagus;
2. Tear the newspaper into strips about 2 cm. in width;
3. Dip these strips into white glue to which water has been added. The white glue should have the consistency of skim milk;
4. Pull the newspaper through your first and middle fingers to remove the excess glue;
5. Wrap the glued strip around the aluminum foil model, until no foil is evident;
6. Use newsprint as the last layer to wrap around the model, as this will make decoration easier; (Newspaper ink will often bleed through the paint if this step is not added)
7. When dried, decorate your sarcophagus, in the tradition of ancient Egypt.

Egyptian Tomb Paintings

Time Frame: Two 40 minute periods

MOTIVATION:

When introducing the culture of ancient Egypt, be sure to make the students aware of the style of portraits done, showing profiles of faces with the eyes drawn from the front view. Review how the Egyptians adorned their heads with wigs and jewelry. In this lesson, the children will produce self-portraits in Egyptian style.

MATERIALS:

- Black indelible fine point markers
- Tempera paint
- Drawing paper
- Water
- Brushes in varying sizes

WHAT TO DO:

1. After discussing with the children the proportions of the human face, demonstrate how to draw a large side view of a head;
2. Show how to sketch the face lightly in pencil, and to fill most of the page;
3. Add details to the drawing in the form of wigs, jewelry and adornments;
4. Have the children paint their portraits in tempera, noting that the Egyptians used brown or beige for the face and green, blue and red for crowns or headgear;
5. When the portraits are dry, have the children outline the painting with the black fine-tipped markers;
6. For a special touch, have the children add details with gold or silver sparkles.

Tet Blossoms

Time Frame: 40 minutes

MOTIVATION:

The Vietnamese New Year is known as Tet, an abbreviation for "Tet Nguyen Dan" or first day. It is celebrated in late January or early February. Tet is a time when people try to catch up on things that they may not have done during the previous year. Bills are paid, borrowed items are returned, and all disagreements are forgiven and forgotten! Blossoms symbolize the rebirth, and welcome spring. In this activity, create a vase of new beginnings blossoms!

MATERIALS:

- Scissors
- Stapler
- Glue
- Brushes
- Magazines (optional)

- Small jar or bottle (baby food jars or juice bottles work well)
- Pipe cleaners or thin wire

- Tree branch
- Plaster of Paris

- Tissue paper cut into squares (about 10cm.)

WHAT TO DO:

1. Demonstrate for the children how to decorate the baby food jar or juice bottles by gluing pieces of magazine pictures on the outside of the jar;
2. Allow to dry;
3. While the bottle or jar is drying, stack 3 tissue paper squares on top of each other;
4. Fold the squares like a fan;
5. Staple the centre of the fan;
6. Carefully pull the tissue paper layer apart;
7. Using the pipe cleaners or thin wire, attach the blossoms to the branch;
8. Mix the Plaster of Paris to a consistency of thick cream;
9. Have the children hold their branch in the jar or bottle while Plaster of Paris is poured into it;
10. Hold the branch in place until it is set in position;
11. Enjoy a year of good luck with your Tet blossoms!

The Road to One-point Perspective

Time Frame: 40 minutes

MOTIVATION:

Showing how object appear at relative distances is called one point perspective. Points and lines give the illusion of three-dimensional objects on a two-dimensional surface. This activity combines very well with a math lesson on line segments. Teachers might wish to prepare their students for this activity by having them look down a road outside the school to notice that objects far away seem smaller.

MATERIALS:

- Drawing paper
- Pencil
- Ruler
- Eraser
- Colouring materials

WHAT TO DO:

1. Demonstrate for the children how to place their paper in a "landscape" position;
2. Measure from the top of the paper about 10 centimetres and draw a horizontal line at that position;
3. Find the mid-point of the horizontal line, that will be the vanishing point;
4. Measure about 3 centimetres from the bottom right and left corners of the paper, and make a dot;
5. Joint the dots at the bottom with the vanishing point. This will create a "road";
6. Along the road, draw trees, telephone poles, fences, etc, gradually getting smaller as they near the vanishing point;
7. Along the top of the horizon line, draw a city;
8. Colour and add details to the one-point perspective drawing!

DISCUSSION:

Once the children have learned how to draw perspective, discuss with them how to make two roads intersect. (This will need two vanishing points)

Complementary Colour Choices

Time frame: 40 minutes

MOTIVATION:

Complementary colours are colours that are opposite each other on the colour wheel. After completing the exercise on creating complementary colours, the children will put their knowledge to use.

MATERIALS:

- White drawing paper
- Small pieces of construction paper in each colour on the colour wheel

WHAT TO DO:

1. Fold a piece of white drawing paper in four;
2. Demonstrate for the children how to make a random design on a piece of coloured construction paper;
3. Repeat this random design on three more pieces of complementary coloured construction paper;
4. Place the cut out designs on the drawing paper rotating around the centre point;
5. Glue in place.

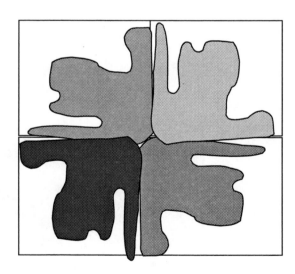

February Art Lessons

Try these art centres:

❖ Make an observational drawing of a desk.

❖ Paint a picture using yarn dipped in paint.

❖ Paint with water on coloured tissue paper on top of white paper.

❖ Practise colouring a colouring page using only different shades of red.

❖ Create a picture using different colours of plastiscene.

❖ Hang a garland of hearts and doilies around the classroom

❖ Make a door hanging by gluing lace and hearts to a construction paper panel.

Graduated Cut Outs

Time Frame: 40 minutes

MOTIVATION:
Learn about hues and shades with this activity.

MATERIALS:
- Strips of construction paper in many colours
- Scissors
- Glue
- Bristol board

WHAT TO DO:
1. Discuss with the children the concept of lighter and darker shades of a colour;
2. Demonstrate for the children how to arrange the strips of construction paper from lighter to darker;
3. Glue the strips vertically across the Bristol board;
4. When the glue is dried, have the children draw a simple shape on the back of the Bristol board;
5. Cut out the shape;
6. Turn the piece over and admire the lovely variations of colour;
7. Glue on a piece of construction paper. (Optional)

TEACHER TIP:
Use simple seasonal shapes such as hearts or shamrocks or Christmas bells.

I Repeat, I Love You!

Time Frame: 40 minutes

MOTIVATION:
This activity repeats a pattern of hearts, using contrasting colours.

MATERIALS:
- Construction paper in white, red or pink
- Scissors glue

WHAT TO DO:
1. Demonstrate for the children how to stack two pieces of construction paper on top of each other;
2. Fold the stacked paper in half, lengthwise;
3. Cut heart shapes along the fold;
4. Cut out the heart shapes again leaving a small border along the cut out space;
5. Fold the final piece of construction paper into 4 lengthwise;
6. Glue the cut out shapes vertically in each of the panels on the final piece of construction paper.

TEACHER TIP:
Use simple seasonal shapes such as pumpkins, shamrocks or Christmas bells for repeat patterns at other times of the year!

Huichol Paintings

Time Frame: Two 40 minute periods

MOTIVATION:

In the city streets of Mexico, lovely yarn drawings may be found decorating walls, straw items and personal accessories such as purses and wallets. These art pieces are bright and colourful. In this activity children will create yarn paintings, as in the Mexican Huichol yarn paintings.

MATERIALS:
- Pencils
- Construction paper
- Glue
- Scissors
- Yarn (thickest is best)

WHAT TO DO:
1. Demonstrate for the children how to sketch a simple drawing in the middle of the construction paper;
2. Using the glue, spread a bead of glue around the outline of the drawing;
3. Carefully place the a length of yarn into the bead of glue;
4. Fill in the remainder of the picture, spreading glue and laying in the yarn until the whole shape is filled in;
5. Make a border around the picture by laying lengths of yarn around the edges of the picture;
6. Fill in the area between the drawing and the border with strands of yarn in different shapes and colours.

Ceremonial Masks

Time Frame: 40 minutes

MOTIVATION:

Aboriginal peoples used masks in many of their celebrations or ceremonies. Today masks are still used all over the world during religious ceremonies, festivals, or celebrations. In this activity, the mask is made from Bristol board, but masks can be made from leather, bark, cloth, grasses, or metal.

MATERIALS:

- Bristol board
- Colouring or painting materials
- Hole punch
- Wool yarn or raffia
- Stapler

WHAT TO DO:

1. Demonstrate for the children how to sketch a large oval on the Bristol board;
2. Inside the oval, draw designs and colour or paint these areas;
3. Draw facial characteristics, such as the nose and eyes;
4. Cut around the bottom of the nose, and lift forward;
5. Cut out the eye areas;
6. After embellishing the mask with designs, punch holes around the edges;
7. Attach wool, yarn or raffia through the holes by folding the wool, yarn or raffia in half;
8. Slip the middle through the hole and then through the loop;
9. Attach two longer pieces of wool or yarn on each side to tie behind the head.

March Art Lessons

Try these art centres:

❖ Make an observational drawing of a hand.

❖ Glue tissue paper pieces to a slick surface (wax paper, foil pie tins, etc). Allow to dry and peel off. Add pipe cleaner details.

❖ Practise colouring a colouring page using chalk and set it with hairspray.

❖ Create a picture using cutouts from a magazine.

❖ Recreate a postcard using markers, crayons, or paint.

⬛🍁 Suzanne Brind'Amour

Time Frame: Two periods of 40 minutes

Susanne Brind'Amour is an artist from Rigaud Quebec. She works in paper mache or tufstone, to create her sculptures. Her sculptures are said to be expressions inspired by movement. For examples of Brind'Amours' art, visit:
 http://www.arte-factum.com/1sba.html

MOTIVATION:
In this activity, children will have the opportunity to create a paper mache sculpture.

MATERIALS:
- White glue
- Paper towel
- Aluminum foil
- Tempera paint
- Brushes

WHAT TO DO:
1. Demonstrate for the children how to use the aluminum foil for the base of the sculpture;
2. Sculpt a bird, flower, or other simple shape;
3. Once the aluminum foil is pinched and shaped into a satisfactory model, dip strips of paper towel into a 1:1 glue and water mixture;
4. Wrap the strips around the aluminum foil shape;
5. Allow to dry;
6. Paint.

DISCUSSION:
Have children share and discuss each other's sculptures.

Shading to Create 3-D

Time Frame: 40 minutes

MOTIVATION:

In this lesson children will learn to create 3-dimensional shape by shading and contouring their drawings. A display of objects that are spheres, cubes, cones, pyramids or cylinders will make references to those shapes more concrete.

MATERIALS:

- Colouring materials (coloured pencils or crayons are best)
- Drawing paper
- A 3-D shape for reference

WHAT TO DO:

1. Teach the children how to carefully examine their object;
2. Look for lightest and darkest areas;
3. Look for places the light shines;
4. Demonstrate how to sketch the shape of the object lightly on the drawing paper;
5. Show the children how to begin where the object is darkest;
6. Choose a colour and LIGHTLY shade in the shape;
7. Press less and less on the colouring material as you near the lightest area of the object;
8. Leave some white to show the highlighted area;
9. Repeat the technique smoothing over the colour, and adding layer after layer of colour, until the object is shaded as desired;
10. Deepen the darkest area of the shape by using the darkest value of the colour chosen or black;
11. Add a shadow extending form the object and colour it black or grey.

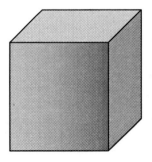

DISCUSSION:

What would happen if the source of light was changed? How would changing the colouring materials make the picture look different?

Picture Making - Drawing People

Time Frame: 30 – 40 minutes

MOTIVATION:

In this lesson the children will be exposed to the simple form of an oval as the base for drawing techniques.

MATERIALS:

- Pencils
- Paper
- Erasers

WHAT TO DO:

1. Discuss with the children the how the human body may be looked upon as "connected sausages". Show how the arm can be divided into three segments, one for the hand, one from the wrist to the elbow, and one from the elbow to the shoulder;
2. Brainstorm with the children where they see other body segments;
3. Model for the children how joining simple sausage shapes may be developed into the human form by drawing the segments and them erasing the lines between the joints;
4. Distribute pencils and paper and allow the children to experiment drawing body forms.

DISCUSSION:

How can this oval or "sausage" be used to make other things?

Picture Making - Review

Time Frame: 45 minutes

MOTIVATION:

The focus for this lesson is to reinforce the concept of the most important part of a picture or the centre of interest, and adding related objects to the background. Children should be encouraged to be inventive and to create scenes that display an understanding of the concepts introduced. For example painting a spaceship in outer space, a fish in the ocean, a dog in the park etc.

MATERIALS:

- Liquid tempera paint (12 colours)
- Assorted paint brushes
- Newsprint
- Water can
- Newspaper

WHAT TO DO:

1. Brainstorm with children possible ideas for the theme of their picture;
2. Review the idea of centre of interest, and adding details;
3. Demonstrate that painting should be done with ends of the bristles of the brush and the handle of the brush should point straight up;
4. Encourage children to experiment with the different textures that can be created with their brush.

DISCUSSION:

Ask children to talk about their picture and discuss the elements of design that they used.

For example:
1. When you painted the fish in the ocean what shapes did you use?
2. How do you know that certain things in your picture are far away?

Glue Resist

Time Frame: 40 minutes

MOTIVATION:

Just as crayons resist a paint wash, glue has a similar effect. In this activity, students will be impressed with their ends results!

MATERIALS:

- White glue in squeeze bottles
- Thinned tempera paint
- Drawing paper
- Brushes

WHAT TO DO:

1. Demonstrate for the children how to drizzle the white glue from the squeeze bottles onto the drawing paper;
2. Allow to dry;
3. Paint over the dried glue with tempera paint to which water has been added;
4. Allow the paints to blend and bleed together, creating a stained glass effect.

TEACHER TIP: Tinting the glue with black tempera paint will simulate leading on stained glass.

Lascaux Cave paintings

Time Frame: 40 minutes

MOTIVATION:

One of the most important archaeological finds in the XXth century was the discovery of the cave paintings at Lascaux, France. A large tree had fallen several years before. A hole appeared where the tree had been and three teenage boys went on an adventure through the hole that would change history. Over 30,000 years before, large red cows, bulls, black stags, and yellow horses had been painted on the cave walls! To visit the caves of Lascaux, go to: www.culture.fr/culture/arcnat/lascaux/en/

In this activity, children will recreate the primitive art of the cavemen!

MATERIALS:

- Brown paper bags
- Crayons
- Tempera paint wash in brown or black (Create the wash by adding water in a 1:1 ration)

WHAT TO DO:

1. Demonstrate for the children how to tear the brown paper bag open to create a larger working surface;
2. Draw a cow, bull or stag on the bag;
3. Colour using crayons;
4. Scrunch the bag into a ball;
5. Flatten the bag and paint over the surface with brown or black tempera paint wash.

DISCUSSION:

Compare the primitive art found at Lascaux to the art produced by the class.

April Art Lessons

Try these art centres:

❖ Make an observational drawing of an Easter lily flower arrangement.

❖ Paint a picture using crumpled newspaper.

❖ Practise colouring a colouring page using pastels. Fix with hairspray.

❖ Trace 4 hands on white paper and cut out. Lay the in the shape of a butterfly, and decorate.

❖ Paint a picture. Place a layer of plastic wrap on the wet picture and lift the plastic off. Make a print using the plastic.

Easter and Earth Day Activities

Puffy Eggs

Have children cut oval shapes from construction paper. On the oval shape using water-based markers, instruct children to create interesting line patterns (e.g., jagged, wavy, thick and thin.) Trace over the water based marker with white glue to produce a puffy effect.

Eggs To Dye For!

Have children carefully draw designs on hard-boiled eggs using a crayon. Dip the hard-boiled eggs into dye baths created with food colouring, water and a bit of vinegar. As an alternative to food colouring, use jelly powders or crystal drink mixes diluted with water.

Earth Day Bird Feeders

Collect pinecones. Coat pinecones with peanut butter or suet. Roll the coated pinecones in birdseed and hang in a nearby tree. Watch for the feasting birds.

Earth Day Collage

Have children create collages using magazine pictures of animals and natural resources such as water. Once the whole paper is covered, encourage children to find and cut out words or phrases to promote Earth Day awareness. For example, "Stop Pollution" or "The Earth is for everybody".

Paper Cut Designs

Time Frame: 40 minutes

MOTIVATION:

During the celebration of Easter ornate paper cut outs or wycinanki (vee-chee-NON-kee) are a part of Polish tradition. The usual cutting tools are sheep shears, still used by paper cutters today. This activity is a wonderful way to incorporate this Polish tradition and a math lesson on symmetry.

MATERIALS:

- Construction paper
- Chalk
- Scissors
- Glue

WHAT TO DO:

1. Demonstrate for the children how to fold one piece of construction paper in half length-wise;
2. Using a piece of chalk, make a design on the fold of the paper;
3. Carefully cut out on the chalk line;
4. Unfold the paper;
5. Glue the design to a contrasting shade of construction paper.

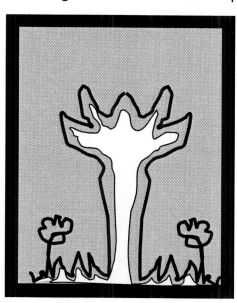

Button-eyed Fly

Time Frame: 40 minutes

MOTIVATION:
Flies have compound eyes that make them hard to catch. They see almost all around in a circle. If you were a fly your eyes would be the size of basketballs!

A study of insects makes this a fun activity. An easy way to demonstrate compound eyes!

MATERIALS:
- Aluminum foil
- Thin wire
- Foam ball
- Straight pins
- Newspaper
- Scissors
- Glue
- Netting or tissue paper
- Buttons or sequins of all shapes, sizes and colours

WHAT TO DO:
1. Demonstrate for the children how to crumple up paper in two sections to form a body and thorax of the fly;
2. Attach the foam ball by wrapping the body in thin wire and joining the head to it;
3. Make two loops at either end of a long section of wire in the shape of wings;
4. Cover each section with netting or tissue paper;
5. Wrap the wire around the body of the fly, securing the wings by twisting at the join;
6. With straight pins, attach buttons and straight pins to the foam ball;
7. Hang the giant fly from the ceiling!

Merry-go-round

Time Frame: Two 40 minute periods

MOTIVATION:

Three-dimensional art can be fun to create when you make things go 'round!

MATERIALS:

- Two large cardboard circles
- Paper towel tubes
- Pipe cleaners
- Drawing paper
- Scissors
- Tape
- Paint
- Glue
- Brushes
- Water
- Miscellaneous item for decorating (glitter, fabric, felt, ribbon, etc.)

WHAT TO DO:

1. Demonstrate for the children how to cut slits around the ends of the paper towel tubes in 2 centimetre depths;
2. Fold these sections out to make tabs;
3. Attach the tabs to the centre of one cardboard circles using tape;
4. Repeat the process with the remaining tubes and attach them in equal distances from each other, around the edge of the first cardboard circle;
5. Repeat to attach the other cardboard circle making the merry-go-round base;
6. Decorate the base with decorating materials at hand;
7. On drawing paper, outline an animal you would find on a merry-go-round;
8. Colour and decorate the animals;
9. Twist two contrasting colours of pipe cleaners together to make the pole;
10. Tape the animals to the pipe cleaner poles;
11. Position these poles inside the merry-go-round, and secure with tape.

Crayon Paper Batik

Time Frame: 40 minutes

MOTIVATION:

Batik is a textile technique. Hot wax is painted on a cloth in a design or picture. The wax is cracked and the cloth submersed in a dye bath. Layers of wax and dye create interesting crackled effects through out the cloth. In this activity children will create the same effects using paper and paint.

MATERIALS:

- Crayons
- drawing paper
- Newspaper
- Water in a large tub or sink
- Tempera paint wash (Paint and water in a 1:1 ratio)
- Brushes

WHAT TO DO:

1. Demonstrate for the children how to apply pressure to the drawing paper creating a thick coverage of crayon;
2. Have children draw and colour a picture on the drawing paper;
3. Ball up the picture to crack;
4. Open the picture and crunch and ball it up again;
5. Flatten the picture;
6. Paint a coat of the tempera wash over the picture;
7. Gently submerse the picture in the tub of water;
8. Wash off the paint;
9. Lay the wet picture on newspaper allowing to dry.

May Art Lessons

Try these art centres:

❖ Tape thin wire along the outline of a bird or butterfly. Glue a second bird or butterfly over top. Once dry, bend the wings in "flying" poses.

❖ Cut a spiral out of cardboard, and suspend objects at intervals down the spiral to produce a mobile.

❖ Paint a picture using feathers.

❖ Cut hands from coloured construction paper and curl the fingers around a pencil Glue several hands to a piece of construction paper and splatter paint or glitter around them to create fireworks!

❖ Cover a piece of paper with a masking tape design and colour all over the paper.

❖ Fill a margarine tub with food colouring, dish soap, and water. Have children blow bubbles in the mixture using a straw. Place a piece of white paper on top to "catch" the bubbles!

Sightless Contour Drawings

Time Frame: 40 minutes

MOTIVATION:

Contour drawings are made when only the edges or outlines of the shapes you see are drawn. There is no shading. Contour lines show the edges and outlines of shapes. In this activity, have fun concentrating on the object while blindly sketching the contours!

MATERIALS:

- Drawing paper
- Pencil
- Interesting objects to draw
- A large book to block view of the object

WHAT TO DO:

1. Set up a large book or divider so the object to be drawn is one side and the paper to draw on is on the other; (taping the paper down makes it easier)
2. Demonstrate for the children how to place their pencil in the middle of the paper;
3. Begin to sketch the object very slowly without looking at it;
4. Do not lift the pencil from the paper;

DISCUSSION:
How would the drawing be different is you could see the object you are drawing?

Say it with Flowers

Time Frame: 40 minutes

MOTIVATION:

On Mother's Day mom will be so surprised by this bouquet! Attached to each pompom is a note with a special message!

MATERIALS:

- Construction paper
- Tissue paper in 6 cm. squares
- Pipe Cleaners
- Stapler
- Scissors
- Strips of writing paper
- Pencil

WHAT TO DO:

1. Demonstrate for the children how to stack 3-4 pieces of tissue paper on top of each other;
2. Fold the tissue paper stack accordion fashion;
3. Wrap a pipe cleaner around the centre;
4. Carefully separate each piece of tissue paper, creating a little blossom;
5. On the writing paper write a job or sentiment for Mom;
6. Attach the strip of paper to the blossom using the pipe cleaner as a tie;
7. Fold a piece of construction paper into a large cone;
8. Insert the blossoms, strips down;
9. When Mom removes a blossom, she gets a special surprise!

TEACHER TIPS:

Some ideas for the job strips: sweep the kitchen floor; breakfast in bed; hug and kiss; unload the dishwasher; wash your car, etc.

Portrait of the Human face

Time Frame: 40 minutes

MOTIVATION:

The math principal of proportion is not an easy concept for elementary students to understand. In this activity, students will be asked to study the placement of facial features.

MATERIALS:
- Drawing paper
- Pencil
- Eraser
- Crayons or other colouring materials

WHAT TO DO:
1. Demonstrate for the children how to fold their paper into 16 squares;
2. Using a pencil, sketch a semi-circle in two of the bottom boxes;
3. Continue the semi-circle in the two boxes directly over the bottom boxes, creating the shape for the face;
4. Have the children study the shape of their neighbours eyes. Point out that the eyes are slightly oval, not round and part of the eye is almost always visible;
5. Sketch two oval shaped eyes on the middle line in the face;
6. Have the children again look at their neighbour's eyes to determine the iris, and its placement under the eyelid;
7. Have the children examine their neighbour's face to focus on the placement of the nose;
8. Point out that the tip of the nose is half way between the eyes and the chin;
9. After studying the face once more, lightly sketch the lip outlines;
10. To make a neck, demonstrate frt the children how to follow the line out from the lips to the edge of the face;
11. Begin to sketch the neck from this position;
12. Notice how the ears begin opposite the eyes;
13. Have the children sketch the ears from the eyes to the bottom of the nose;
14. Half way between the eyes and the top of the head is where the hair begins;
15. Complete the portrait by adding details to the picture.

Japanese Carp Kites

Time Frame: 40 minutes

MOTIVATION:

Kite flying plays an important part in Japanese culture. May 5 is the Boy's Festival. A carp kite is the symbol of courage, and is flown for every boy in a Japanese family. In this activity, stuffed carp can be flown over the classroom.

MATERIALS:

- Large tracers of fish
- Craft paper
- Paint
- Markers
- Newspaper
- Wool
- One-hole punch
- Optional: glue & sparkles

WHAT TO DO:

1. Have children trace a large carp fish shape onto a folded piece of craft paper;
2. Next have children cut out the fish shape;
3. Model for the children how to use the scissors to cut out scales.
4. Glue on scales and sprinkle with sparkles, or decorate with markers;
5. Demonstrate for the children how to hold the fish pieces together and staple the fish at the nose and tail;
6. Punch holes around the fish and have children "sew" the fish sides together, leaving an opening;
7. Remove staples and stuff the fish with newspaper;
8. Finish sewing the opening used to stuff the fish;
9. Display the stuffed fish by hanging them from the ceiling.

Chinese Scrolls

Time Frame: 40 minutes

MOTIVATION:

Artists in China used brushes made from bamboo and animal hair. The animal hair bristles were drawn to a fine point to enable the artists to paint lovely flowing pictures. Black ink made from pine soot and glue was the material of choice. Sometimes vegetable dyes were added to the paintings to produce fine colours. Paintings were done on silk scrolls and rolled for safekeeping. In this activity, children will have the opportunity to try Chinese scroll painting.

MATERIALS:

- Shelf paper
- Black tempera paint
- Thin brushes
- Pencil
- Ribbon (optional)

WHAT TO DO:

1. Each child should be given a piece of shelving paper;
2. Demonstrate for the children how to lightly sketch a Chinese symbol on the shelving paper using a pencil;
3. Some choices might include a dragon or fish;
4. Outline all the parts of the symbol with black tempera paint;
5. Allow to dry;
6. Roll the scroll and tie with a ribbon.

June Art Lessons

Try these art centres:

❖ Make an observational drawing of a bicycle.

❖ Paint a picture using thick and thin paintbrushes.

❖ Practise colouring a colouring page using mixed media.

❖ Draw a picture of your family.

❖ Draw a picture with white glue on black construction paper. Sprinkle with salt and allow to dry. Shake off excess salt and hang!

❖ Twist brown tissue paper into "branches" and glue on cherry blossoms by pinching squares of pink tissue paper in the centre.

Monochromatic Style

Time Frame: 45 - 60 minutes

MOTIVATION:

Monochromatic means using one colour. In this activity student will choose one colour and draw a picture using different intensities of that colour. Encourage the children to choose crayons or pencil crayons rather than markers, as it is more difficult to create a variety of tones in marker.

MATERIALS:

- Drawing material
- Paper

WHAT TO DO:

1. Discuss with the children the elements of composition, such as foreground, background and focal point;
2. Demonstrate how to lightly sketch a scene of their choice on the drawing paper, using one colour;
3. Show the children how to create depth and contour by shading the picture. Pressing on the crayon or pencil to acquire darker colours, rather that choosing a darker crayon or pencil, may do this.

Pin Art Luminaries

Time Frame: 40 minutes

MOTIVATION:

Dress up plain old lunch bags to look like works of art. The end product of this activity makes a lovely luminary for summer backyard decor.

MATERIALS:

- Construction paper
- Push pins
- Newspaper
- Masking tape
- Lunch bags
- Magazines (optional)

WHAT TO DO:

1. Have the children choose a simple picture form a magazine or sketch a design;
2. Make a pad of newspaper;
3. Place the lunch bag on top of the newspaper pad;
4. Attach the picture or sketch to the front of the lunch bag, using the masking tape;
5. Demonstrate for the children how to push the pins around the edge of the design or picture;
6. Puncture through the lunch bag into the pad of newspaper at about two centimetre intervals;
7. When complete the bags can be filled with about 10 centimetres of sand and a small candle placed inside;
8. This makes the bag glow and shed a lovely pool of light.

DISCUSSION:

Pioneers used this process to make tin punched lanterns. Why would these be used in that time period? Can you find other countries where luminaries are still be used for festivals? (Mexico)

Honey Bee Good!

Time Frame: 40 minutes

MOTIVATION:

Over 20,000 species of bees exist, but only the honeybee makes products we use! The honeycomb is built in an old tree, or in special hives developed for honey collection.

In this activity, turn your classroom into a hive of activity, or use it to develop a math concept on octagons!

MATERIALS:
- Construction paper
- Glue
- Wool or yarn
- Paint
- Colouring materials
- Pencils
- Tissue paper
- Tape
- Brushes

WHAT TO DO:
1. Demonstrate fro the children how to draw a hexagonal shape onto the construction paper;
2. Show how to extend each side of the hexagonal shape to make a square, with a triangular shape between each square;
3. Cut each on one side only;
4. Fold that triangle into the square shape;
5. Fasten each side with tape, to form a hexagonal comb;
6. Glue the combs together to form a large honeycomb, and paint yellow;
7. Demonstrate for the children how to draw a bee, using black and yellow colouring materials;
8. Attach tissue paper wings and using the wool or yarn, hang the little bees inside the honeycombs!

Caution Bleach at Work!

Time Frame: 40 minutes

MOTIVATION:

Bleaching out areas on construction paper can be an effective way to demonstrate negative and positive space. In this activity, caution children not to get bleach on their clothing or other areas where it could do damage!

MATERIALS:

- Construction paper
- Cotton swabs
- Bleach
- Smock or plastic raincoat to protect clothing

WHAT TO DO:

1. Before beginning the activity, dilute the bleach in a 1:1 ratio with water;
2. Demonstrate for the children how to dip the cotton swab in the bleach and water mixture;
3. "Paint" the bleach on the construction paper, often dipping the swab in the bleach;
4. Allow to dry.

DISCUSSION:

Discuss with the children the positive and negative spaces created by the bleach.

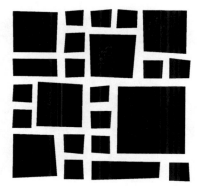

Rangoli From India

Time Frame: 40 minutes

MOTIVATION:

Rangoli is an art technique learned by girls in some Indian homes. The art form is passed down from generation to generation. Decorating the floors with rice flour mixed with water is usually done for celebrations. The mixture is drizzled through the fingers to form intricate designs. The designs are temporary and wear off in a few days.

MATERIALS:

- Flour
- Water
- Tempera paint
- Wax paper
- Tubs to contain mixture

WHAT TO DO:

1. Before beginning this activity mix flour and water together to form a thin mixture;
2. Demonstrate for the children how to scoop a handful of flour and water out of the tub;
3. Drizzle the mixture onto a sheet of wax paper;
4. Leave undisturbed to dry;
5. Once dry, dip fingers into the tempera paint, and paint between the drizzles!

DISCUSSION:

How does your family prepare for celebrations or special events?

Assessment and Evaluation

Artist Portfolio and Journal

An artist portfolio with a journal, is an excellent way for children to organize their thoughts and ideas about the art concepts presented. Grammar, spelling, or syntax in the journal entry should not be emphasized. The student responses give the teacher opportunities to plan follow up activities that may review and clarify concepts learned. In addition, a portfolio is a wonderful keepsake to show off a student's artistic abilities.

Art journal entries may be done intermittently depending on scheduling. Entries should be brief. Time allotted for completion should be less than fifteen minutes. Entries can be done with a whole group, small group or an individual.

Art Journal Entries can include:
- Direct instructions by the teacher;
- Key ideas;
- Personal reflections;
- Questions that arise;
- Connections discovered;

Thinking About My Art

In my artwork, I did a good job on:

_____

Next time I would like to:

_____

My Artwork Plan

Name of art project: _____

I am going to use the following art materials:

Crayons _____   Pencil crayons _____   Paint_____

Construction Paper____   White Paper _____   Other _____

Thinking About Art

Name of art project

_____

This piece of art makes me think about:

_____